The Traveler

The Traveler

A Book of Prose and Poetry by

Mohammad Bader

www.Lulu.com

Copyright © 2011 by Mohammad Bader

All rights reserved. No part of this publication maybe reproduced in any form or by any means, electronic, mechanical, photocopying, recording or otherwise, without the written permission of the author.

Printed in the United States of America

Cover and Interior Design by Lulu

Jerusalem Photos by Fotolia.com

ISBN 978-1-257-01551-1

Dedication

To Jerusalem, with all my heart. May peace reign over your olive orchards and fig trees.

To all of the immigrants and refugees who fled their birth homes, seeking shelter and peace in so many corners of this world.

To Diane, Sarah, and Gabriel, who bring joy to my heart and who bring me back to earth when my head gets lost in the clouds.

To Suleiman and Yusra, who were the symbol of sacrifice, honesty, and perseverance.

Introduction

As a child, I read poetry time and time again. I had ease and facility remembering and reciting it. It was music to my ears. Nonetheless, every time I attempted to write my own poem, I ended up with a conglomeration of senseless sounds. The sounds rhymed, but the words did not communicate an idea of significance to me or to others.

It was not until I became less concerned about rhyme that I was able to express what I wanted without the restriction of rhythmic melody. These poems and prose are the result of an honest and true look at my life's experiences and interactions. They were written in Arabic and English at various periods of my life. Such poetry and prose provided me with peace and tranquility. Being musical was not my objective; choosing big words or using complex vocabulary was not my intent, either. I wrote in Arabic, my mother tongue, and then translated into English. Many poems were written in English first. I found that repetition soothed me and healed my soul. Therefore, I used repetition. It was not a mechanical process but an intense spiritual experience. I felt that I was able to get a deeper emotional response when my mind slowed down and repeated a concept. There is a huge advantage to that and to getting in touch with my own feelings. I use poetry to know myself better and to know those around me.

These selected poems were written over a period of more than twenty years in my life before and after I arrived to the United States. I chose to divide this book into four different themes: Part I is on Love and Man-Woman Relationships; Part II is on Peace versus War; Part III is on The Immigrant and the Motherland; and Part IV is on Utopia versus Morbidity.

As a newcomer to the US, I was struck by the cultural difference between man-woman relationships and love, a very different and sensitive subject. These poems symbolize the man-woman relationship as a complex subject, and I am not going to attempt to explain it. I had to learn how to negotiate and establish partnership with the women in my life. Having gone to all boys' school as a child, I did not know how to behave around women until I entered college. Even then, relationships were very constricted and formal. As a new comer to the US, it was very exciting to engage in a friendship with women and to experience love. My initial relationships were rocky as I brought with me that old thinking. As I learned to share power, I realized that my relationships improved.

I am very fond of the work of William Blake and Khalil Gibran, particularly concern with social justice and inequity caused by social statuses. I am also drawn to the aspect of their work that depicts dichotomies and bipolar opposites. As humans, we are torn and tormented with such extremes. We go to the extremes to avoid pain in relationships. We go through stages, and to me the most important stage is not the honeymoon period but the longevity of a relationship. Are relationships worth fighting for?

The theme of Part II is Peace versus War. Competition makes animals of us. Fighting for natural and geopolitical resources makes savages of us. We don't see the other side as human. Basically, we see the enemies. Until we see each other as fully human and vulnerable, we may never achieve peace. I pray for PEACE to win.

The theme of Part III is The Immigrant and the Motherland. This theme addresses the agony and the frustration of a man's search for justice and freedom from all forms of oppression. Naturally, an oppressed person travels to democracies to find respite from injustice and tyranny. This book addresses an immigrant's trial to break free from one culture to try and adopt another culture in the United States. Making the step to leave family and friends behind is a very tough one to take. Here the call from Motherland is a tough one to ignore. The immigrant tries hard to assimilate and looks for support. Torn by the past, perplexed by the present, and apprehensive about the future, the immigrant's relationships are seemingly difficult. Also, there is a whole set of ideologies and philosophies that are different and are not appreciated equally by other newcomers to the new land.

The theme of Part IV is Utopia versus Morbidity. There is a farce in the land of opportunity and freedom. Such a land promises the newcomer a new concept of greater hopes and expectations, promises of success and plenty—a man-made heaven. In reality it is nothing but a glamorous facade that eats the newcomer alive. The utopia is created as a mixture of perfect dreams and fulfilled hopes, money, love, success, and freedom. But the traveler is reminded of the cold existential fact that a man is born alone, and will die alone. In this man-made heaven, man hides all of his morbid feelings and compensates for that fear of finally being alone.

Finally, some of these poems and images came to me at intense moments in my life. Some of those moments were happy and some were sad. I hope you can find yourselves or someone you know in these poems. They are meant to draw us together through the commonality of our human experience.

Mohammad Bader

Contents

Part I:	**Love Man-Woman Relationships** 1	
	When the Sun Sets.. 2	
	My Sweet Valentine... 4	
	My Love 6	
	Where Are You?.. 8	
	Bilateral Deception 9	
	Silence..11	
	Eulogy: A Letter to a Friend 13	
	Eulogy: A Letter to Mother.................................14	
	Mother and Son...16	
Part II:	**Peace Versus War** 17	
	Scream 18	
	A Dream 19	
	Night Owl 20	
	Satisfaction..21	
	Neighbor or Cousin 23	
	News...25	
	Hebron..27	
	Palestinian-Arab 29	
	Jerusalem 1 33	
	Jerusalem How Can I forget you?.......................34	
	Destiny...36	
	Perhaps 37	

Part III:	**The Immigrant and the Motherland**	**39**
	Cross the Border	40
	The Traveler	41
	A Mother's Call	45
	Ahmad, the Arab	47
Part IV:	**Utopia Versus Morbidity**	**49**
	The Merciless Wind	50
	Great Hopes	52
	Perfection	54
	Loneliness	55
	After All	56
	Christmas Music	57
	Meditation	58
	Rain	59
	A Bird	60
	Lost	61
	Insomnia	63
	Forceful passion	64
	This Is My Life	65
	Whispers	66
	Night Owl 2	68
	The Night	69

PART I
LOVE MAN-WOMAN RELATIONSHIPS

When the Sun Sets

When the sun sets,
My shadow disappears,
And so does yours.
My heart travels to the dejected past
To numerous years ago...
To decades of...
Isolation and mysticism.

When the sun sets,
My shadow disappears;
And then,
I live alone;
I feel alone;
And I can't but
Think of you.
Who are you?
I do not know.
What is your color?
I do not know either.
What are you?
I also do not know.
Something attracts me to you,
Maybe the unknown!
Or maybe a desire that roams in my heart.
I wish I knew who you were.
I wish our shadows met.
I wish you knew that I
Searched for you... for many years.
Until now you have never come...
Will you come, please?

عندما تَغيب الشمس
عندما تَغيب الشمس...يختفي ظلي و تَختَفين
يرحل قلبي الي بعاد السنين...
الي عصور المعتزلة والمتصوفين
عندما تَغيب الشمس... يختفي ظلي...
وحينها... أعيش وحيداً...
وأشعر بالوحده...
ولا استطيع الا ان افكر فيك
من انت؟ لست ادري
ما لونك؟ لست ادري
ما انت؟ ليت ادري....
شي يشدني إليك...ربما المجهول
او ربما رغبة تجول في خاطري
اود لو ادري من انت
أود لو ظلينا نَلاقي
الا تعلمين أني بحثتُ عنك عبر السنين
والي الان لم تأتين
تعالي...رجاءاً!

My Sweet Valentine

I love you from the longest distance,
I love you from the closest distance.
Your eyes: two charming pearls,
Your eyes: a symbol to the universe,
Brown and bewildered
Like my bewildered heart.
Your smiles heal my aching heart.
Oh, lady of beauty,
I love thee.

Oh, lady of warmth
And gratitude,
Musical lady,
A lady in an existential world:
You knock on my door
And compose music
To my loving and lost heart...

Oh Lady,
You are sweet, and
Beautiful...
Your radiance
Attracts me to you...forever

Oh, my love!
I am yours and you are mine forever.
And on this beautiful occasion,
I wish you the best Valentine.

في عيد الحب

احببتُك من بعيدا
واحببتُك من قريبا
عيناك لؤلؤتان ...ساحرتان
وضحكاتُك ...تملي القلب الولهان
عيناك رمز للكون والعلمان
بنيتان وحائرتان... .كقلبي الحيران
يا سيدة الجمال...اعشقَك
يا سيدة الحنان ... والعرفان
يا سيدة في دنيا الألحان
يا سيدة في دنيا الوجدان
ياسيدة تَطرق الباب
وتلحن الأنغام لقلبي الحاير الولهان
انتَ حلوةٌ...
جميلةٌ...
وسحرُك... يشدني نحوك طوال الزمان
يا حبيبتي .. أنتَ لي... وانا لكَ
طوال الزمان...
وفي هذا العيد ...
أتَمني لَكَ احلي الأعياد

My Love

I loved you, love me!
I sanctified you, sanctify me!
I saw you an angel at doomsday
Covering my shivering body
And... Absolving my past sins.
I looked for you while lost, confused.
Not knowing my fate,
I looked for you in my dreams
And in my consciousness
And by all the sentiments
And rosy dreams this universe bestowed upon me.
My love, I look for you every morning:
I trip over your rosy perfumes
And your honey eyes.
My love,
I loved you. Love me!
I sanctified you. Sanctify me!
And I went looking all over the universe and you found me
And who am I but a lunatic
Lost, confused
Flying like rose petals in autumn
Searching for a place
And a home
And a woman to hold me and
To wipe the sins... and the disasters of the time.

حبيبتي

أحببتك... احبيني!
قدستك...قدسيني!
رأيتك ملاكا يوم الحشر... تذكريني
وتمسحي عيوب الماضي
وخطايا السنين
بحثت عنك... تائها ...شاردا
لا اعلم المصير
بحثت عنك في أحلامي ووجداني
وبما ترب علي الكون
من مشاعر واحلام ورديه
أبحث عنك كل صباح
اتعثر برائحتك الورديه
وأحلم بعيونك العسليه
حبيبتي...احببتك...احبيني!
قدستك...قدسيني!
لقد بنيت لك معبدا في مخيلتي
لتبقي معي كل السنين

Where Are You?

Wherever you are my friend?
I miss you;
Whatever your dreams;
Whatever your thoughts;
Whatever place you've been;
The thought of you
Comforts me;
All my troubles disappear
And I move into a mystical paradise;
My thoughts…
And my dreams… are… with you.
My beloved friend,
I miss you!

Bilateral Deception

Don't try to deceive me!
I know your games.
Don't try to sympathize with me!
Your sympathy is a dwindling charm.
You want something from me.
I want something from you.

Both of us need each other.
Both of us deceive each other.

Say it!

Don't hide it!

Why don't you say it?

Frankly,
You and I
Deceive each other

Caution: life becomes semi-poisonous.

خداع متبادل

لا تحاولي ان تخدعيني!
فانا اعلم الاعيبك
لا تتعاطفي معي، فعاطفتك سحر يتقلّب

تريدين شيئا مني
واريد شيئا منك
كلانا يريد شيئا من الاخر
قوليها!
صراحةً... أنا وانت نخدع الاخر
حذاري ...
فالحياة تصبح شبه سامه

Silence

Sweet sounds, then ….silence.
Play,
Joy,
Then, silence.
Life full of joy,
Then, silence.

Silence,
Silence,
Silence,

Mingled with awe,
Mingled with cruelty,
Mingled with calamity,
Silence... and a torture of one's conscience.
Was I mistaken?
Or did I dare to break the chain?

صمت

ضجيج عذب...
ثم صمت
لعب ومرح...
ثم صمت
حياة مليئة بالمسرات
ثم صمت...
صمت...
صمت...
صمت...
ينتابه رهبه
ينتابه قسوه
ينتابه شعور بالوحده
صمت وعذاب ضمير
اهل اخطأ ت أنا
ام تجرأت ان اكسر القَيد

Eulogy: A Letter to a Friend

Long before we met,
I closed the door;
Then I stood like a fool,
Lying to myself.

I was hungry,
But you nourished me;
I was a hermit,
But you brought me to light;
I was not understood,
But you understood me;
I was lost,
But you recognized me;
I was in the dark,
But you set your light upon me;
I was weak,
But you strengthened me;
I was angry,
But you calmed me down;
I was conflicted,
But you brought me peace;
Then, I was numb.
Now I ache.
Then, I did not cry;
Now I sob.
Then, it was hard to say words.
Now, I ramble on forever
My friend, I miss you!
May you rest in peace!

Eulogy: A Letter to Mother

I look at your face
And I see a flaming sun,
Yet, you don't sigh.
I wake up at night
And I hear you moan and cry, softly.
I see you as a candle
That burns silently.
I see you as a volcano
That holds the disasters of the past.
Don't you despair?
Questions come to my mind:
Why are you moaning?
Why are you crying?
What is this buried sadness?
Talk to me!
Talk to me, please!
Narrate to me a myth of the olden days!
And afterwards tell me about your buried secrets.
Forgive me mother, for I am impatient.
Forgive me if I seemed solid as steel.
Today, I feel your sadness in my bones.
Forgive me! That sadness sickened me.
For I learned nothing but moaning.
And as if we were twins whenever you moaned, I did.
When I asked you about the reason,
With a gentle whisper you delete the question.
Until now I wonder:
Why the moaning?
Why the buried sadness?
Don't you despair?
Forgive me mother that I did not understand.

Forgive me for I have not tried.
Your tears shock my foundation,
And your heart was a temple in which I buried my worries and sadness.
Forgive me mother for I did not lift up your pain.
Forgive me that I gave you my burdens.
Now I know the secret of your moaning.
Now I know the reason for the buried sadness
And the silent volcano.
Thank you for being
A temple for my pain and burdens,
A sun that shone,
A candle that burnt silently,
And a volcano that erupted internally.

Mother and Son

You call me son.
I call you mother.
Sometimes we have fun.
Sometimes we run
From each other
And from the world
And from our emotions.
We find ourselves
In different worlds;
But swiftly, we unite.
Nothing destroys our ties.
And nothing will make us lie
A strange composition,
Different complexion;
But true emotions,
And true relation.
Mom, I thank God,
For being your son.

PART II

PEACE VERSUS WAR

Scream

Scream, scream little child.
How I wonder what you hide.
Brilliant pale, frozen tear,
In your eye my dear.

A Dream

I trudged amidst the desert's heat.
Vultures crowded the sky.
The heated wind slapped my face.
Then, I couldn't stand
The heat, the vultures, and the arid land.
Far away I saw an oasis.
I crawled over the sand to lean against a palm tree.
In moments I slumbered
And began to dream.
I dreamt that:
    All nations knelt to the Creator,
    All nations recited a peace song together,
    All nations blended,
    And colors, ranks, and social statuses ended.
    False pride disappeared,
    And white pigeons formed a white flag for peace.
    The flag held the burdens of all the nations;
    And a phrase beneath it said,
    "Freedom for all and justice forever."
I woke up and had to move on.
In the mirage, I saw another oasis
And another dream.
Amidst all:
Vultures,
Heat,
And wind.
I moved on with a desire and a dream,
Carrying an oasis... in my so-called savage heart.
Still I carry a dream.

Night Owl

I am a night owl...
And a restless soul.
Do you hear my cry?
Do you see through my soul?
I left behind a precious jewel.
Amidst a tempest, I lost my jewel.
I look back and
Find nothing.
I look back and
Find destruction.
No peace;
No happiness;
Nothing;
Nothing
But war, everywhere.

Satisfaction

Satisfaction. Give me satisfaction!
Satisfaction is all I want.
Freedom is all I need.
Satisfaction to my soul,
Satisfaction to my race,
Satisfaction to my children,
Satisfaction to my existence.
The soul is restless
And not satisfied, my friend.
I don't see satisfaction in the eyes of the children;
I don't see satisfaction in the eyes of those
Who were robbed in the brightness of the day?
While the world's peace keepers chose to sleep.
Satisfaction, satisfaction is all I want.
Are you satisfied?
Can I find satisfaction?
Where?
Many souls were killed, beaten, and stripped of their dignity.
Did that satisfy anyone?
The greedy satisfied their flesh,
But what about their souls?
Were they satisfied?
You hear about injustice in the West Bank—
Who is satisfied by that?
Are the settlers satisfied?
Physically, perhaps, but their souls shall want peace.
Now tell me who is satisfied?
You are not satisfied, nor am I.
Jerusalem, a paradoxical city,
A city once called the city of peace,

Is the hub of tyranny and injustice?
Do these Arabs count?

Neighbor or Cousin

Neighbor,
Can you call me neighbor?
Are you my neighbor?
Or shall I call you cousin?
Our father is Abraham, but we refuse to share him.
Is your God, my God, cousin?
Or do we only use history the way you please.
Cousin:
I refuse to believe in an unjust God—
A vindictive God,
A God that gives you what He takes from me.
Is my home what your God promised you?
Or are you nothing but thief justifying your murderous crime in the name of God.
My neighbors I empathize with your pain, but do you empathize with mine?
We both live in Diaspora for years and years to come,
And if you insist on your own ways, we shall ever be condemned to a life of Diaspora.
You and I
Shall want peace,
Shall want comfort,
Shall want justice,
Shall want love,
Have you looked into my eyes lately?
Yes, anger is what I feel.
Yes, indignation is what I feel.
Yes, war crosses my mind every second in my life.
For I am fed up with your tyranny,
With your injustice,

With your God
Who gives you what He takes from me.
Yes, my eyes are bloodshot with tears.
Yes, my eyes are filled with sorrow and sadness,
And my heart is blackened with grief.
I see you drive me and my children to the slaughterhouse,
And I have nothing on my hands except shackles and manacles.
And the world peace keepers are watching you silently
Like a voyeur enjoying the scene of a rape.
And who I call my brothers in tongues are in deep slumber
Enjoying the gifts of your God
Then, why do you fear me?
I am nothing but a mirror image of you.
I am as broken as you are.
I am as full of fear as you are.
I long for peace.
I long for a place to call home.
I long for a play ground for my children.
I long for a picnic under the olive trees on the hills of Jerusalem

Shall we make peace?

News

I am tired of reading the news;
I burnt my paper in my fireplace.
When will I hear the good news?

The news
When the roses can no longer be crushed by the monster.

The news
When those who have can no longer dictate the rules.
When will I hear that fire is no longer consuming my Jerusalem?
When will I read that justice has come through?
Paper boy:
Don't deliver me the paper today.
Your paper has no news for me.
I shall mourn and grieve,
And if I talk, I shall be brief.
I shall dress in black
And drink bitter coffee.
I shall raise black flags.
I shall only speak of my tears—
No laughter,
No joy,
No purple suits,
No roses for me
Until the war stops
And till freedom reins in my Jerusalem.
Tell the widows to dress in black!
Tell the orphans to dress in black!
Tell the soldiers to go back!
Tell the politicians to stop the attack,
On the sons and daughters of peace,
On the flowers and the roses,

On the fig and olive trees,
And on the breezy hills of Jerusalem.
Peace,
Peace,
Peace shall come,
War shall end.
When the vultures leave the hills of Jerusalem,
The black flag shall come down,
And the infants
Shall sing with the nightingales.
The fear shall subside;
And love shall preside
On the hills of Jerusalem.
I shall be in mourning until the good tidings,
The good tidings that Jerusalem is free,
And that the vultures have left.

Hebron

I yearn for the starry nights of your grapevine fields on a summer night.
Once we were children and walked all over your hilly plains.
Like fools we walked on for hours:
No busses,
No cars,
No bicycles.
But we walked on foot, anxious and eager to reach to your sweet grapes,
And your plum trees,
And fig trees.
We were young and restless.
We were young and foolish.
We thought of nothing but the moment.
We wanted to run from home to the warmth of your fields,
And we did.
How beautiful that was!
The rocky and rugged mountains, a picture that remains in my mind.
The days of bird watching and listening to the birds chirp
Sent us to a deep ecstasy.
Then, we saw no soldiers,
No guns,
No military jeeps,
No barricades.
Hebron, I am as foolish today as when I was ten:
I miss your grape-vine fields.
I miss your fig trees.
I miss your afternoon breeze.
Far away from me you are.
Now your fields are filled with smoke.

Al-Hassoon no longer chirps,
And has left frightened by the blast.
The grapes are bitter and sour
For they have not seen the sun of freedom.
And the stars waned
For their light was subdued by injustice.

Palestinian-Arab

Apprehensive I feel...
I don't know where to start.
The rage and anger is locked inside.
Driven by passion and crippled by distant emotions,
I hide behind my struggle and I don't know how to come out.
How to have the courage to curse the darkness;
How to stand up and light a candle;
How to tell a story that was told a million times
But never through my tongue, heart, and lips.
Where do I start and how shall I end?
Never able to articulate, I go in circles.
I like a tempest, a volcano, and a squall ...dormant.
But beware when it comes out.
My friend, I shall tell my story.
I shall unlock my lips and my heart.
I shall pour my tears:
Tears of anger,
Tears of fear, and
Tears of years of isolation and injustice.
I was born to a place I cannot call my own.
I was born to a place glorious yet could not hold my soul and tears.
And would not give me hope.
Everything I saw in there made me sick.
Paradoxical land. Beautiful yet sickening.
Holy, yet sacrilegious,
Fervent, yet dull.
My friend,
I am a stranger,
A visitor
Living in this strange land.
However, loved and accepted I am,

I shall be a stranger to the day I die.
I still yearn for my mother land;
My life, my friend, is colored with years of injustice and fear.
Why? I ask.
Was I born with a curse?
Was my neighbor born to a better God?
I hope you get the picture by now.
I am the son of misery; they are the sons and daughters of joy and fortune.
I am the son of poverty; they are the sons and daughters of wealth and excess.
I am the son of the weak; they are the sons and daughters of the strong and powerful.
I am who the world watches for; they are those who are cared for.
Should I say more, my friend?
Did you get the drift?
I shall be clear and succinct
And spare the rhetoric:
I am the Palestinian,
The Arab you forgot and still fear.
You equate me with bombs.
You hear of me only when CNN brings me to your home,
Disfigured,
Maladjusted,
And thirsty for blood.
I am the Palestinian Arab.
The one who you are not sure of.
But if you look into my eyes and ask me,
I will tell you:
No, I am not a sheik.
No, my father does not own an oil well,
And no, I don't herd sheep.
I do not live in a tent,
And I never rode a Camel.
It is true, I pray to a God called "Allah";
Yes, I dress differently.
Should that make me less than you?
Through the years,
You called me names
And cut a deep wound in my heart.

Today, I ask you to join me and dress my wound.
I won't fight or blame you for the damage you have done.
I just pray that our wounds may all heal.
My friend,
I tell you ...
I know that you have watched me bleeding and left me on the side of the road alone.
I tell you ...
That your righteous silence crippled my body and soul.
I tell you ...
That your fear of my face and my religion, made you blind to see me.
I tell you ...
That the way you interpret your holy books put a dagger in my heart.
And using the name of God, you wrote my obituary while I am still alive.
My friend... let's forget all that, and we shall start fresh.
Know me as I know myself!
I am good and humble;
I love to learn and read;
I love people and love to be loved;
I love to have a place to call home;
I like to be respected in the airports of the world
And in every border;
I love to have schools for my children
And a job to feed my family;
I like to travel in my own country without having to carry my passport around my neck.
I like to stroll with my wife and kids
In the streets
Or in the public parkWithout fear and apprehension.
I like to...
Well I hope you get the drift
Because I am tired of trying to prove that I am like you.
I have similar dreams and desires.
Do you get my drift?

Old City Jerusalem-Fotolia.Com

Jerusalem 1

A paradise
I cannot enter,
A dream,
A mirage,
A destiny of destinies.
The whole world wants you
And your children deported from you.
Destiny of destinies,
A morbid existence
To those who love thee,
Your children,
Who walked your streets
Barefooted,
Who hung around your dark and crowded allies,
Those who swept your streets,
And whose donkeys and carts decorated your streets.
And the sound of the peddlers
Shouting,
The hustle and bustle,
All that for what?
A shekel,
A diner,
A dollar? Or just to get by?
A very crowded city, of empty hearts now
Who flooded to you from the entire world to the "chosen land"?
What an irony:
A holocaust nation lives on the debris and the blood of another

Jerusalem How Can I forget you?

People flock to you every day
And talk
And argue
About your history
And culture
And about your lost children.
Those who ran away and run out
And those who dream of you
Awake every night,
Counting the days to come back to you
Jerusalem:
You are a home for those who are lost,
A paradise for those who are away
And to those who are present,
So how can I forget you?

كيف أنساك ياقدس

ثم يأتي الليك البشر...
في كل يوم
ويتحدثون...
ويتجادلون...
عن تاريخك وحضاراتك...
وعن أبناؤك المشردين...
اللذين يحلمون فيك
ويسهرون الليل يعدو الايام والسنين
ليعودو اليك
يا قدس!
يا منزلا لكل التائهين
يا جنة لكل الغائبين
ولكل الحاضرين
كيف أنساك؟

Destiny

Was I supposed to be...
In here?
In there?
Or, somewhere?
Floating like an autumn leaf,
Having no place to call home,
Tossed again and again
By the wind,
Gentle at times,
Fierce and destructive at others
Am I the child of man?
Or am I the child of morbid destiny
Following my crippled path
Seeking fortune and joy
Amidst destruction...

Perhaps

Perhaps…
We walk together
One day.
Perhaps…
We reach the water spring,
And drink the water of freedom.
Perhaps…
We look up at the sky
Blue,
Clear,
And the atmosphere…fine.
Perhaps…
We'll have peace … one day…

ربما

ربما نسير معا
يوما ما....
ربما نصل الي النبع
ونشرب مياه الحريه
ربما ننظر الي السما...
زرقاً...
صافيه...
والجو...هادي

ربما نجد السلام...
يوما ما...

PART III

THE IMMIGRANT AND THE MOTHERLAND

Cross the Border

"Cross the border,
Cross the border,"
A voice whispered.
"Sail away!"
I crossed the border.
Nothing was waiting for me:
A couple suit cases,
A travel document,
A few dollars,
And an optimistic smile.

The Traveler

The Traveler travels to the farthest distance to experience something new—to see something out of the ordinary, far beyond any imagination. The Traveler is like a singer who wishes for stardom and sings a new song. And after it is sung, the singer feels lonely. It is an everlasting and inherent loneliness, the cure for which is to write and sing a newer song.

The Traveler travels the farthest distance, crossing the seven seas, not knowing that at each crossing, he alters something in the depth of his soul.

Thus, the Traveler started his travel. He became sick of the ordinary. He became bored with unproductive sounds. He became infuriated with frigid songs and started to look for newer songs. He began to look for a new garden, an outlet to free his thoughts and to confide in it of his deepest secrets. He traveled far away, as if he wanted to forget his past and start a new beginning. Although the Traveler wanted to forget his past, he was not ashamed of it; he made it a torch to light the darkness of his future.

However, the Traveler changed. His soul changed. He became more aware of the silence and the sorrow that accompanied him since his birth, and he started to think about the oppression he lived under. Back then he did not think of such things. Back then life was harsh and mechanical. No time to reflect. However, now that the Traveler transplanted himself in a strange land, he has more time to reflect and think.

The Traveler sits under a palm tree and finds shelter under its shade from the heat of the summer's sun. He sips a glass of lemonade as the sweat trickles down his forehead and cheeks, when a white-bearded man appears to him. The Traveler was both stunned and elated, for the figure looked comforting and reassuring. The young man spells out what is kept inside of him, and tears come out of his eyes. The wise man looks at the Traveler with kindness and asks him, "What ails you, son?" The Traveler shivers and squints his eyes as tears are about to come out of them, and with a coarse chocking voice he replies:

"There is a transparent, paper-like wall I want to penetrate, but I cannot go through or conquer. I struck it numerous times, and it felt as solid as steel. I gather my strength, I run, I jump and strike it with my shoulders with all might, but I cannot tear it. I cannot penetrate the wall."

I gather my strength.
I jump.
I strike.
Then, I feel numb.
I touch the wall, it feels like steel.
I look in the mirror.
I look at my face.
And I see
Venom and gloom.
Then I hear an echo directed at me,
"Frightened and a coward.
Frightened and a coward.
Frightened and a coward."
My body trembles,
And I hear deep silence.
I look at all directions
And whisperingly, I thank the Creator
That I am alone.
The echo repeats,
"Frightened and a coward,
Frightened and a coward,
Frightened and coward." I become bitter.
I become enraged.
I go ablaze
And feel a flood of broken emotions.
Suddenly, I acquire audacity
And I shout as loud as I can.
"I am not afraid.
I am not a coward."
The echo replies and says:

"Indeed you're afraid and a coward."

The wise man leans forward and looks the Traveler straight in the eye, and softly says, "Conscience makes cowards of us all". The Traveler looked at all directions, looked at his own reflection in the nearby pond, then looked at the wise man and shouted:

"Where is conscience?
Where is the conscience?"
And as tears fell off his cheeks he kept on going and said:

"I'm sick of this life.
I'm sick of this fear.
I'm sick of these chains.
I'm sick of these shackles.
I'm sick of everything.
I feel that I am a captive.
I like to be free.
I like to be free.
I like to be free.
Voices chase me.
They echo in my head
And they hound me.
"Who am I and what the essence of my existence and what do I want from my life?"

The Traveler looks at the wise man and with a remorseful and weak voice begins to say:

"Once again,
I live an artificial life.
I ride a boat driven by a merciless wind.
I ride a boat driven by the storm.
I ride a boat that follows the current.
I am sick of the storm.
I am sick of the current.
I am sick of the wind.
I like to sail against the current.
I like to face the storm and the squall.
I like to race the wind and the rain.

I wish I knew the essence of my soul.
I am still a stranger in a strange land"

The Wise man asks the Traveler: "Then what is the solution, son?"
The Traveler answers:

"I wish I were a monastic monk.
I want nothing.
Not a treasure.
Not a palace."

The Traveler suddenly halts and slows down and he whispers:

"Oh! I live a fallacy."

Then, the Traveler looks like he suddenly acquired a high level of insight and enthusiasm. A glimpse of hope comes through his dark and stern face. His eyes relax, he wears a smile, and he looks at the wise man and says:

"Today, I proclaim I am opposing all the rules.
I will sail alone,
Opposing all currents,
Opposing the wind, and
Facing the storms.
I will sail against the wind and the storms.
I will sail against the wind and the storms".

A Mother's Call

Mother,
Mother,
Mother, I hear you call my name from all directions.

"Son,
Son,
Where are you, son?"

I hear you saying:
"My beloved son, how long will you be estranged,
And when will you return home?
You are far away me my son!
And I am waiting for you!
I have not changed a thing in your room.
I dust it.
I dust your books and pictures
And your lonely lute.
Perhaps you forgot your family,
And forgot your home,
Or perhaps your life in the West kept you busy.
Son, despite the absence of your visage, your spirit is with me.
Don't be late! How long will you be gone?
My beloved son, when will your journey end?"

Mother, I hear your voice call my name from all directions.
Your voice is the key that opens my heart
And dissolves the rust and decay of my estranged heart.
Mother, here I am.
Mother, I am coming to you.
Mother, here I am.
Mother, here I am.

I shall be, some day, coming back to you.

"When?"

I do not know!
Mother,
I need your big heart,
And I am lost without your compass.
Mother,
You're my light house and my garden.
You're my Eden and Euphrates,
You're my Nile and Jordan
And, I shall carry you in my heart,
In life,
And in my hereafter

Ahmad, the Arab

Don't ask about my name and my address,
For the night and the stars are my brothers and sisters,
And the planets of the world are my companions,
And the will of God protects me.
I have lost my family and friends,
Wandering weary in this foreign land.
I have asked the night to hold me,
To hold me beneath its wings,
And the stars guided me to my eternal garden.
I am Ahmad, the Arab.
I am looking for a shade and a garden.
I am searching for a home and an address.
I am searching for a friend and a human,
And I search for identify and citizenship,
And I chase after a passport
To justify in it my humanity to those who oppress me.
And I have taken from
This foreign land,
A shelter
To my children,
To my beloved,
And to myself.
And I wandered far away,
Stranger in a strange land,
Burying my pain and my sorrow.
In this huge distance
Do not ask me about my name and my address.
For the night is my house,
And the stars are my lanterns,
And back East I have a home,
That calls me every morning.

لا تسألني عن اسمي و عنواني
فالليل والنجم إخواني
وكواكب الدنيا ترافقني
ومسيرة الله ترعاني
فقدت اهلي وخلاني
وهمت في بلاد الغرب أشقاني
سالت الليل بجناحيه ان يطويني
والنجم أُرشدني الي خلد بستاني
أنا احمد العربي
ابحث عن ظل وبستان
وابحث عن بيت وعنوان
وابحث عن خل وإنسان
وابحث عن جنسية وهويه
واطارد خلف جواز السفر
لأبرر فيه انسانيتي لظلام
واتخذت من الغربة ملجأً
لاطفالي واحبابي وكياني
وهمت غريبا وحيدا
اواري في الغربة الامي واحزاني
لا تسألني عن اسمي و عنواني
فالليل منزلي
والنجم مصباحي
ولي في الشرق منزل
يناديني كل صباح

PART IV
UTOPIA VERSUS MORBIDITY

The Merciless Wind

The wind carries you without mercy.
It folds you,
It surrounds you,
And transfers you to a hell you don't know.
In spite of that,
You enter hell with a torch of hope:
Hopes,
Songs,
And musical dreams.
You search all means of comfort.
Magically, hell transforms to heaven,
A heaven made by your hands.
You ornament it how you please—
Bring maids and mermaids.
After a while you start to admire
Something called ecstasy.
Life becomes like a wheel,
Events repeat,
And ecstasies numerate.
History repeats itself time after time.
Then, the soul wonders, what does it want?
Ecstasy after ecstasy after ecstasy
No? It is a shock!
Renders you numb;
Spacey,
Floating in emptiness.
When ecstasy vanishes,
You feel strange;
You feel bitter;
You feel anger.
Life becomes like water,

Without taste, smell, and color.
You try to hold on to anything
That gives you hope.
The wind comes again.
It carries you without mercy,
It folds you,
It surrounds you,
And transfers you to another hell.
Congratulations! You are a step ahead
Once again:
You create wonders from hell;
You build dreams,
And float in emptiness.
After all ecstasies are over,
Without doubt,
You'll still feel strange
Once again:
The wind carries you without mercy,
It enfolds you,
It surrounds you,
And throws you to a hell you don't know.

Great Hopes

These great hopes
And great desires
    To aspire
        To acquire
Is an illusion that eats you...
    Like fire.
Do you still aspire?
    Or is it that you
    Like fire?
I see you burn with passion
Climbing the highest mountain
Climb,
Climb,
Climb,
Then—take a breath, and
    Look up,
    Look up,
    Then, look down.
Are you high or are you standing still?
"Standing still," I hear you say.
Moving up, yet feeling immobile?
Like a patient on stretcher
Asking "When can I move?"
You say
"Up!
Up!
I want to wake up."
You say
"Move,
Move,

Move." You say
"Try better.
Try harder,
Try something new."
Oh, my God, I tried so many.
I don't know what will be coming next.

Perfection

Along the way:
I'm walking along the way
With all my shortcomings, trudging away,
To come close to you and to my perfection.
It's so tedious, my friend.
I'm afraid I'm not able to hold on that perfect dream of being perfect.
I'm not perfect, and I accept it deep in my soul;
I accept my humanity.

Along the way:
I'm walking along the way
With all my shortcomings I'm trudging away.
Trudging to you and to my perfection.
A bit closer perhaps.
A bit better perhaps.
More exact, more sharp, perhaps.
Lighter, brighter, shorter, and narrower perhaps.
All the adjectives, perhaps, my friend.
I'm trudging heavily to fulfill a dream, my friend.
The roses I have planted died.
The pictures I took came out dark.
The paintings I started are not finished.
The colors, perhaps, were dimmer than they should be.
It's so tedious, my friend.
I'm afraid I'm not able to hold on to that perfect dream of being perfect.
Finally, I admit it.
I'm not perfect, and I accept it.

Loneliness

An old black horse among thousands of white yearlings, gazing sadly at the sky;
An owl singing *tu-whit, tu-who* and nobody replies;
An abandoned hut in the lonely desert, waiting for a single night-comer;
An old mother waiting for a fighting son to come back home;
An eagle grasping a crag, ringed with the azure world;
A philosopher spending nights deliberating about the secret of existence;
A worshipper crouching all night, watching the rise of the dawn silently;
An artist drawing the moon in a calm summer night.

After All

After all, you shall depart your soul.
Thrown in a dark narrow hole,
You shall sleep alone.
Whether you like it or not,
You cannot fuss about it.
After all, it's all you have,
All you own.
It's nothing but
A dark hole
A chilly humid tomb
After all, you shall
Sleep alone.

Christmas Music

Another Christmas comes by;
Another place to run by.
Perhaps more treasures;
Perhaps more pleasures
Upon a day when every soul
Cannot run away.
You come to my day,
And make it bright,
And make it light,
And move me into your fantasy land.
Christmas may not have been for you and me.
We may never believe in Santa,
But what I believe in is that my spirit lifts up
When I hear the music of Christmas.

Meditation

Oh Lord,
Comfort me!
Oh Lord,
I abide in Thee.
Oh Lord,
Comfort me!
Oh Lord,
I worship Thee.
I appear lost my Lord
From that lesson you taught me
That left me humble

So counsel me!
Without you Lord,
There is no me.

Rain

Drip…
Drip…
Rain drops fall upon my lips.
Drip…
Drip…
The north wind chills my hips.
Swish…
Swish…
Water splashes all over my chin.
Hazy,
Daisy,
Today is cloudy and breezy.
Tomorrow will be shiny and rosy.
The weatherman has gone amuck:
He took sunshine and locked it away.
So let's pray
He'll bring it back
On a rainy day.

A Bird

I am a simple man
With a simple mission.
Simplest things make me happy:
A bird looking for a feed,
Singing,
Dancing,
Mating and prancing
Caught my sight
And brought
Delight
To my heart.
Flying high and twittering away,
She left plenty of joy to color my day.
I am a simple man
With a simple mission.
Simplest things make me happy.

Lost

Don't think me lost!
Don't call me
From behind the fog!
Don't pull me
By a thread hanging from the clouds!
Don't hold my hands
From behind the fog!
For, I am
Lost,
A vagabond.
I sing to the world,
And the world sings to me.
I live my destiny,
And go my way.
Clouds chase me,
And fog envelopes me.
And behind the fog,
An endless road
I walk and walk.
I disappear, and disappear.
And don't know: where is my final destination?

ضائع

لاتحسبني ضائع
لا تناديني من خلف الضباب
لاتشدني بخيط معلق من فوق السحاب
ولا تاخذ بيدي من وراً الضباب
فانا شارد و متجول
أناشد الدنيا...وتناشدني
أعيش في قَدري...
واستمر في امري
سحاب يطاردني
و ضباب يلفني
وخلف الضباب طريق بلا نهايه...
امشي وامشي...
اختفي واختفي
ولا اعلم الي اين المصير؟

Insomnia

Severe insomnia,
Then insomnia.
Where from?
Don't know—
Scruples of mind
And the mind:
Rebellious,
Awake,
Fumbling in this world,
Chasing a mirage.
What does man think of after he fulfilled his animalistic instincts?
After man fulfills the illusion of accomplishment,
What does man think of?
Homeland?
Family?
Friends?
Humanity?
God? Or a Higher Power?
Or the destruction that accompanies the world?
Or of orphans, who wander amidst destruction?
The tears from a child's eye leave us with one question:
Why?
Tell me my friend!
What should a man think of?
When you come to bed, at night,
You close your eyes shut, and when the world is asleep
All your senses awake in your body.
You wish you were a machine with an on/off button.
Turn it OFF! Turn it OFF!
Or you can stay awake and spend the night with the angels.

Forceful passion

This forceful passion,
This calamity,
Serenity,
And clear vitality.
The human animal in us
Tamed,
Demure,
Swift to cry,
Swift to hit,
Swift to judge,
Swift to fight,
Swift to do anything to fulfill that ...
Animalistic passion.

This Is My Life

This is my life.
I love it
With its disaster
And originality
And beauty and elegance
And by the legends I read
And by the rain storm that drowned it
And by the torturous storms that tore it.
This is my life: temporary, borrowed
Life started rough,
And perhaps it will end rough.
This is my life, and I am not the maker of it.
It followed me
And befriended me,
Built me and destroyed me.
It's all I have.
And who am I?
Dust, water,
And a soul had blown into a fragile flesh.
A borrowed life,
And I am not the maker of it
And when my soul departs my body
Nothing remains but dust,
A dust that will scatter.
This is my life.
And despite of its harshness,
I love it
As is
By its purpose and futility
By its frankness
And by all that which is difficult.

Whispers

When the sun sets
And when the stars light the sky
Like candles,
And when the wind
Accelerates, playing beautiful musical melodies—
And when tranquil quietness
Envelopes the whispers,
Then I sing whisperingly and dance;
I gather all my senses,
Which brings me closer to the creator.

همسات

عندما تغيب الشمس...
وعندما تضي النجوم السما...كالشموع
وحينما تتسارع الرياح
وتعزف موسيقي عذبة
والهدوا الساكن
يلف الهمسات
حينها اغني "همسا"
وارقص واستجمع كل الحواس
التي تقربني الي البديع

Night Owl 2

Night comes,
Darkness settles, and
Extreme cold
Thoughts float in space,
Looking for a lost star,
And looking for a moon to light the darkness,
And looking for fire to warm this sad heart.
Night comes, and all secrets awake.
Everybody is asleep, except the night owl,
Sad and lonely.
None befriended her except a dimly lit moon
And a few scattered stars,
Which disappear behind the heavy fog.
The night owl gives her secrets to one of the stars
And goes to sleep, and the next day, she does the same:
She gives the moon and the stars her secrets, then goes to sleep.

The Night

The night is my friend,
My lover;
My suit
That covers my body
And my shortcomings.
A lover that keeps my company,
A hound that chases me,
A priest that comforts me,
A nightmare that awakens me,
A brook that quenches my thirst,
A mirage that keeps me thirsty,
A blessing that follows me,
A misfortune that shocks me,
The night is my friend and lover.
The night brings me closer to the Creator!

الليل... صديقتي... وعشيقتي
والليل بدلتي التي تغطي جسدي
والتي تخبئ عيوبي واسراري
الليل... منتجعي ومأواي
الليل... سرابي... وحسابي
الليل يواري الآلام واحزاني
الليل يضمني...يحتضنني
كعاشق... يأنسني
كشريد... يطاردني
كقديس... يوانسني
كحلم... يسليني
ككابوس... يفزعني
كنبع... يروي ظماي
وكسراب... يزيد عطشي
الليل نعمة تلاحقني
ونقمة ...توقظني
الليل صديقتي و عشيقتي
الليل...
يقربني الي البديع

Mohammad Bader 71

About the Author

This is Mohammad's first published book. Born in East Jerusalem, a stone throw away from the Dome of the Rock, Via Dolorosa (Latin for Way of Suffering), and the Western Wall, Mohammad spent much of his early life interacting with international pilgrims and tourists. Bader started his travel to the USA with the idea that he will be trained to become a counselor. Shortly after he arrived to the US both of his parents died and the first Palestinian Intifada (uprising) started. Mohammad was later adopted by his sponsor, Bettie Mitchell, founder of Good Samaritan Ministries International. Mohammad participates in poetry reading and will be happy to read his poems in person and talk about his experience as a recent immigrant. Mohammad has chosen Portland, Oregon and the USA to be his permanent residence. He hopes for peace and justice He can be reached via e-mail at thearabiantraveler@gmail.com or at http://thearabiantraveler.blogspot.com/.